A Vision

Inspired By

The Heart

First Edition
3-4-14

Leanna Gay

Copyright © 2014 Leanna Gay

All rights reserved.

The Author holds exclusive rights to this work. Unauthorized duplication is prohibited. No part of this publication may be reproduced, distributed, transmitted in any form or by electronic or mechanical means including information storage and retrieval systems, without the permission in writing from author. The only exception is by a reviewer who may quote short excerpts in a review.

First Paperback Edition: January 2014

The opinions expressed in this manuscript are solely the opinions of the author. The Author has represented and warranted full ownership and/or legal right to publish all the materials in this book.

Blog: http://www.leannagay.blogspot.com

ISBN-13: 978-1494283889
ISBN-10: 1494283883
LCCN: 2014901789

DEDICATION

To my loving husband Ricky. You are my inspiration and I am truly thankful for all you have done and do. You give me the strength and courage needed to make a difference in anything I do. .

CONTENTS

	Acknowledgments	I
1	Vision of Destiny	Pg # 1
2	Through the Storms	Pg # 8
3	Mother's Inspiration	Pg # 10
4	Life's Healing Light	Pg # 17
5	Beauty Serenity and Compassion	Pg # 21
6	Essence of the Heart	Pg # 27
7	Light a New Beginning	Pg # 33
8	Inspirations of Art	Pg # 38
BIO	About Author	Pg # 45

A Vision Inspired By The Heart

A Vision Inspired By The Heart

A Vision Of Dreams
To Be Inspired
By Destiny
By Leanna Gay

A Vision Inspired By The Heart

ACKNOWLEDGMENTS

To all my family and friends, I would like to thank you for all your encouragements for helping me stay on task. I hope that all that is written in this book will touch your lives and give you the inspiration that it has given to me. For the heart of compassion is filled with the inspiration that comes from within.

A Vision Inspired By The Heart

A Vision Inspired By The Heart

CHAPTER 1
Vision of Destiny

My Vision

My voyage began in my hometown of Moultrie, Georgia. From within comes a dream full of compassion and love. From a poet, a novelist emerges to embark on an adventure of a whole new fantasy. Never lose sight of what you can become because from within, you can create your own destiny. My journey is a Vision To My Own Destiny.

A Vision Inspired By The Heart

BENEATH THE CLOUDS
AS THE LIGHT
COMES TO LIFE

A Vision Inspired By The Heart

Dreams Verses Reality

In a dream you are persistent to get to the end. Some dreams never end. Some dreams you can make a reality. Some dreams you write about and make your own ending. In life, you are persistent in your goals. In life, you can make your goals a reality. In life, you can make your own ending. What you pursue is what you can become. Be yourself, don't lose sight but make the most of what you can do. You will be surprised in what the outcome can be if you only try.

A Vision Inspired By The Heart

A Vision To Your Own Destiny

For a path you choose is the beginning of what is to come. One purpose filled with compassion and strength. A fantasy comes to life with a vision fulfilled of a destiny beyond anything imaginable. Believe in the wisdom of what you can achieve. Believe in yourself for your strength comes from within. You control your own path of a Vision to Your Own Destiny.

By: Leanna Gay 11-05-13

A Vision Inspired By The Heart

Arise For Your Path Is Unique

A mind full of wonder, a vision to see,
Life filled with purpose, one to surmise,
So full of compassion, the heart soaring free,
Finding strength, deep from within you will arise,
For what lies ahead, with your head held high,
A beacon to others, for a light you shall be,
Words wisely chosen, with wisdom to comply,
Intent of the reason, desired from within me,
With a purpose in mind, driven to inspire,
Life beyond measure, as a destiny unfolds,
Time stands still with a balance to acquire,
A heart remains as the future upholds,
Confident and precise, dare to belong,
Bound no longer, set free to believe,
Driven by desire to be radiant and strong,
A time, a place for you to achieve,
Remember your purpose so you will be effective,
For everything you do will be at its peak,
Above and beyond with life's perspective,
From within you arise, for your path is unique…
By: Leanna Gay --09-03-13

A Vision Inspired By The Heart

Light Your Way

Remember the Light when a storm arises. You never know what lies ahead. For one path is stormy like there is no end in sight. The other path leads to hope in the light. As the light breaks free through the clouds you see, feel the warmth of a calming peace for this path laid out is a guiding light. Have the courage to find your strength. From within give hope to others in the mist of the storm. Light Your Way.

A Vision Inspired By The Heart

Silence, Purpose and Destiny

Silence is not an option when the hurt is greater,
We look at the past and wonder why it is,
As we go forward, we wonder what is to come,
Pray for the weak, pray for the strong,
and it will get better,
Taking each step, as you put one foot forward,
Though the path may be long, and you may stumble
Not knowing how, with a hurdle to get through,
With a purpose in mind, you push onward
As needs arise, you look, you see, you will be humble,
Time will pass as you proceed in good times or bad,
If you fall and if you should fail,
What is to come, is not known,
You push forward and learn from them all,
Rise up, defeat it and you will prevail,
Time is of the essence, wasted by many,
Look to the horizon, you will be amazed,
Make a choice, Learn to listen, linger not,
Become surreal, from the battle within,
take control of our own destiny.

By: Leanna Gay – 7-21-13.

A Vision Inspired By The Heart

CHAPTER 2
Through the Storms

As The Storm Arises

As the storm arises, no end in sight,
The clouds rage on, will there be light?
As the skies darken, the rains commence,
The lightening begins, and the rains intense,
As the thunder rolls, the hail begins,
The winds pick up, will this end?
As the funnel forms, the end is near,
In the blink of an eye, the skies are clear,
As the clouds break, the sun will form,
Let peace be still, In the mist of a storm.
By: Leanna Gay 6-4-13

A Vision Inspired By The Heart

Finding Your Path:

Strength, Courage and Endurance is a path in the road you travel. Have the Courage to find your way through any obstacle. Weathering a storm to find your path can be a rocky road. Finding the calm within a storm takes endurance. If you have been through it, you have the courage to withstand it. If you find a way to overcome it then that takes courage. God gives us the strength to endure what was, what is and what is to come. God gives us the courage to overcome any obstacle. Ask for guidance and have the faith to pursue the path that is before you, so you can endure what is to come.

CHAPTER 3
Mother's Inspiration

Songs Of The Mind
Inspiration before the Poem

When I wrote this poem, I was reflecting on a difficult time in my life. We lived with my grandmother and I loved staying in the living room especially when the wind blew. You see when my mother passed away she lay in the casket in that same place. The night after she was no longer there, the wind blew. Through the wind, you could here the violins play. At that time, I never heard them until after she was gone. Yes, it was a sad time but many years later, I realized that it was also a happy time. You see, as I looked back music filled the room as if it was a comfort, a peace and a calm after the storm. For that is how I will remember and how I choose to see it. I will say that it was the neatest thing to hear. Here is the poem I wrote as a reminder.

A Vision Inspired By The Heart

Songs Of The Mind

Songs of the mind to the violins' tune,
Day by day, not a moment too soon,
A melody of love's pure delight,
Within an existence, light shining bright,
Days will come, as harmony will flow,
Eyes closed to listen as soon you will know,
Air filled with music as the songbirds fly,
Morning dew comes, now the sun is high,
Wind is howling, as the violins play,
Mesmerized by song to show you the way,
Reaching within, guided by light,
Shared in a thought, willed by might,
Dreams by night, lives fulfilled,
Hearts will sing, as the tune will build,
One life as we know it, one moment in time,
Music filled hearts to the sound of a chime,
United as one forever, you will see,
As the Violin plays, so soothing it will be....

By: Leanna Gay 09-14-13

A Vision Inspired By The Heart

A Mother's Gift

A love for my mom is special to me,
As I remember the special times we had,
She drilled in us values of what we can be,
Whether or not in good times and bad,
As the love in her heart has always shown,
I will cherish them always so that I see,
That she is not forgotten and always known,
Our Moms are special as that should be,
Her heart of love with lots of wisdom,
As she has lifted me in so many ways,
She helped so many not knowing the outcome,
As she was a blessing and amazes me always,
To know my mom was the best,
She has inspired me and continued to uplift,
As she was loved, she was kind and she was blessed,
This in itself was my Mother's Gift.
By: Leanna Gay 5-17-13

A Vision Inspired By The Heart

Mom I Love You!!!

How special is my mother to me,
As I say I love you each and every day,
To dance, to run, to listen and to see,
What each day will bring I dare say,
Each day I go to school to learn,
To read, to write and being attentive too,
My mother awaits, for my return,
In the morning, I tell my mom I love you,
And off to school and on the bus I roam,
Classroom filled as the kids start to flock,
As I board the bus to go home,
To my puppy I wave and then a big shock,
The first to go with tears in my eyes,
To my Grandmother's house I now go,
As I say goodbye hurt and cries,
To another house, I have to follow,
As the house fills and the people pile in,
For what comes, I do not know,
To the news, I find myself within
As I am told yet of another sorrow,
To my knees I go as my cries go out,

Leanna Gay

My second to go, heavy and hollow,
As I take a day to play and shout,
I ponder, I think, as I see her lay,
As I ran outside to pick a red rose too,
With tears in my eyes,
I give her the rose and say,
To my Mom I so love you....
By: Leanna Gay 05-15-13

A Vision Inspired By The Heart

A Cry From Within

As you go about day in and day out,
You see outwardly and want to fit in,
While on the inside, you fight with conflict,
Look and see what it is all about,
You take a walk, down a trail,
With the quiet and calming peace,
You listen to the sounds all around,
In and around you awaken to sail,
Flying freely on eagles wings,
High above with the wind on your back,
As you descend below you prevail,
Captivated you listen as it sings,
In a crowd, you're shunned and dismayed,
But soaring in the clouds there is peace,
To your surprise, they include you,

Leanna Gay

Only to make an example you feel betrayed,
Dazed and confused as you go into a backspin,
Your hurt is beyond measure as you try to breathe,
Needing an answer, needing some comfort,
All you can see is a Cry From Within…
By: Leanna Gay 7/22/13

CHAPTER 4
Life's Healing Light

Life is what you make it to be. You will go through obstacles. You will go through changes. Everything is a mystery of what life has in store. Take it as it comes. Acknowledge it, deal with it, learn from it and you will find that life's mystery can become what you make it to be. How you perceive it, how you learn from it and how you deal with it will give you the paths you choose. Choose your path. You can make it worse by dwelling on it or you can make it great by accepting it and moving on. Search inwardly; find what is needed for the choice lies in the hands of the beholder. Take a chance and make it a great one. Only you are in control of it.

A Vision Inspired By The Heart

Heal It & Seal It:

Healing is to put your past in the past,
Go forward, you never forget
but remember what is,
To deal with it, to learn from it, to live at last,
A memory forever and forever will miss,
Life is too short to dwell on what was,
Whose fault it is, it matters not, learn to forgive,
Learn to start over,
Take the first step just because,
Accept it, deal with it, only then can you begin,
No matter what is in store, to see it,
For your wounds to be healed, from within,
The day will come for the time to commit,

A Vision Inspired By The Heart

Doing this with love will help heal the heart,
Time without measure, to accept and admit,
Memories forever present and will never depart,
For the heart to heal it, only then can you seal it.
By: Leanna Gay 04-27-13

A Vision Inspired By The Heart

Driven By Hope There Is Light

Driven by circumstances no one knows,
The loss of a loved one so tender it shows,
The grief takes over and you cannot see,
Overwhelmed and confused inside you flee,
Day by day, night after night within your bounds,
All of your struggles in your mind it surrounds,
A fate unforeseen and nowhere to hide,
With a cry from within trying to decide,
No where to turn to, with your whole being in dire,
From the inside, looking out your soul afire,
The need for a companion, the need of a friend,
To hear, to listen with their heart to lend,
Time stands still, no relief in sight,
Inward you're lost, from within you fight,
Life is in turmoil, hopeless it seems,
A friend in need, inside of your screams,
No one to lean on, no way to cope,
The need to overcome, driven by hope,
One day at a time, from a glimmer of night,
Unforeseen is the way, for one that remains,
There Is Light.
By: Leanna Gay Written on 09-01-13

CHAPTER 5
Beauty Serenity and Compassion

Captivated Heart

Dreams are a beauty of which can't be seen,
Deep are your thoughts, in a field of green,
Images of the mind in which you behold,
Inspired by stories that are sought and told,
Shimmer of light, sunlit rays from above,
From within your heart, feelings of love,
For one you can see and one you can feel,
Sunlight is to see, from the heart you can heal,
Time is irrelevant, every moment to live,
Each day a reminder, a need to forgive,
Meadows of peace as the wind blows,
Air filled with warmth as the breeze slows,
Visions of the mind, thoughts that are new,

For a future unseen, and imagine it too,
Envision a time that can never depart,
A promise from one to another is a
Captivated Heart...
By: Leanna Gay – 09-22-13

A Vision Inspired By The Heart

Serenity of Light

In a pasture filled with nature, beauty of such wonder,
Calmness fills the air surrounded by splendor,
Filled with a peace from within as it now resides,
Slowed in motion in a measure time, as the dew abides,
On the horizon the awakening begins,
mesmerizing to me,
Power of beauty, glisten with delight,
as my eyes can see,
Light caressing my face as it peaks through the trees,
Illuminating the warmth, soothing to know how it feels,
Water flowing rapidly as the solitude surrounds me,
Perfection before me behold the radiance I see,
Nothing but sounds and glare of the sun seeps through,
My eyes closed as I let my mind go,
to see all things new,
From within is greatness,
completely filled in tranquility,

Listen, learn and believe, surround yourself endlessly,
From the one that truly sees,
for their purpose that awaits,
As the vision of splendor for that of such grace,
Through the path of contentment allured by my sight,
Radiance captivated before me is the
Serenity of Light...

By Leanna Gay 10-26-13

A Vision Inspired By The Heart

Compassion of the Heart:

Expressions perceived by people are always in different ways. Be a friend, be a listener, be the hope and a guidance to others. Shine a light unto others so they can see the Compassion of Your Heart.

A Vision Inspired By The Heart

One Moment In Time

Walking a path, though beauty surrounds me,
Dewdrops have fallen with the sun that is rising,
Array of hope, light shining through the tree,
Wind is blowing, though it is not compromising,
Streaming at a glance of the rivers flow,
Wild and untamed, as the eagle takes flight,
In the wind as they fly with the fields below,
Through the fields as fast as I might,
Gradually I come to a perfect surrounding,
Through the trees, on my face the sun breaks free,
My mind is racing and my heart is pounding,
Amazed by sight of what I can see,
Taken by the light that is stunning and glistens,
Compassion of the one standing before me,
Emotions start rising, to the one that listens,
Sensation of the touch, Hearts running free,
Essence of splendor, sensations anew,
Mountains before me thoughts of the mind,
Astounded by the beauty, so radiant and true,
Enchanted by sight, One moment in time...

By: Leanna Gay 09-20-13

CHAPTER 6
Essence of the Heart

Soul Afire

Softly, tenderly a kiss to begin,
Two hearts, two souls, the flame that burns,
Rhythm of the beat, a race within,
Emotions fly, a desire that yearns,
My heart, my soul I give you this night,
Wildly Raging filled with exhilaration,
Denied no longer, radiant with sight,
Intertwine we are, with stimulated sensation,
Elation of need, from within commence,
Fulfilling and glowing, as passion unites,
Embracing the moment, so blissfully intense,
Raptures of bliss, when passion ignites,
A burning desire, igniting within me,

Leanna Gay

My life I give, my love shining bright,
Into the abyss, forever we will be,
My Soul Afire, my love's pure light.
By: Leanna Gay 08-31-13

A Vision Inspired By The Heart

Passion Embraced

Locked inside is a desire from within,
A soul that burns two hearts of one mind,
To him I belong as I yearn to begin,
A flame ignites, beating hearts intertwined,
Eyes to see deep from within, sealed with a kiss,
So much love, uncharted time, to you I bring,
Loves desire, passion of flame, my heart of bliss,
As we go forward my heart that sings,
So pure and innocent, that moment in time,
Endless rage, excite and commence,
As one we share, the higher we climb,
Glimmer of rapture, blissful and intense,
Tenderly, softly blended with exhilaration,
Delightfully overtaken and joy to acquire,
A moment in time with stimulation,
Passion Embraced Of Loves Pure Desire…
By: Leanna Gay 8-25-13

A Vision Inspired By The Heart

Heart of Souls

Intertwined to be, in remembrance to thee,
A time we had, what we have and what will be,
Intertwined together, our hearts to remain true,
Tender is the touch, as the trickle of morning's dew,
Intertwined in one fluid motion,
one time one place,
Heartbeats faster, as one unites and embrace,
Intertwined in a dance of the moonlit night,
Eyes glistening in the rhythm of morning's light,
Intertwined moment as the cold becomes heat
One fluid movement to the drum of the heartbeat,
Intertwined by might with the glow of light,
Motion of balance in the flow of the night
Intertwined as the flame flickers and consoles,
As one intertwined, to be the Heart of Souls…

By: Leanna Gay 10-28-13

A Vision Inspired By The Heart

A Passion Rekindled

As I sit day by day, I ponder the thought,
Bliss uncharted, with my soul afire,
Flashes, images, and dreams I had sought,
The need arises to my hearts desire,
Intertwined to you, myself I am placing,
My eyes filled with the twinkling of light,
A moment in time as my heart is racing,
Tied up in knots with the glimmer of sight,
My heart, my love, my desire freely given,
Passion unites to the sound of your beating heart,
No time has measure for us to live in,
Unified we stand and never apart,
From within the rage, two souls become one,
To you I belong as the fire dwindled,
Two hearts, two souls as now it is done,
Overtaken by joy, with a Passion Rekindled.
By: Leanna Gay 09-24-13

A Vision Inspired By The Heart

Light Of The Dance

Music begins as you move your feet,
Intertwined together to the sound of the beat,
Beginning and end as one we will face,
From one to another in a time to embrace,
Set in motion as the music will build,
Twirling faster as no one will yield,
Rhythm to the sound, swift as might,
Within a trance to the flickering light,
Relentless, unwavering, one thought one mind,
A beauty of wonder so caring and kind,
Slow is the motion in an endless bliss,
Flow is the tempo as in time will not miss,
Captivated is the moment, surrounded by romance,
Perpetually binding in the Light of The Dance
Written By: Leanna Gay 12-28-13

CHAPTER 7
Light a New Beginning

Hope In The Light

Challenges of life, there are many,
Overcoming, they can be complex,
Pressures building if there are any,
Frustrations commence time can reflect,
Thoughts are racing, nowhere to turn,
Struggling within with no way out,
Conflict within intense is the burn,
Don't let it consume you and be without,
Complication is how you perceive it,
For there is a way, find the will,
Fill your heart and never submit,
Pray if you must and let your heart fill,
For the pressure will lift one day at a time,
To help you realize your true prospective

There is hope within the light, a time to climb,
Make it worthwhile, so it will be effective,
As the frustration starts to diminish,
Strength from within shining bright,
Pressures subside as they begin to finish,
Complexity of life becomes the
Hope in the Light.

By: Leanna Gay 09-15-13

A Vision Inspired By The Heart

Love's Holy Light

Light shining down as the stillness lies,
Clouds roll in as the fresh rain descends,
Sounds of wonder as the beauty arises,
Showers of splendor until the finale ends,
Morning of glory so fresh and new,
Skies open up with a breath of fresh air,
The gentleness of the breeze as the wind blew,
Radiance allured scattering abroad to share,
New growth appears as the earth restores,
Birds singing with wings spread wide,
Running wild and free as the eagle soars,
Rivers race to where the still waters reside,
Stunning is the beauty from where I stand,
Eyes closed, dreams of wonder only I can see,
Time stands still in the wake of a command,
Unveiling of time remains a mystery,

As the Clouds depart, remember the feeling,
Surrounded by splendor alluring to sight,
Fascinated by vision of a mountain revealing,
As sunlit rays shine through to
Love's Holy Light....
By: Leanna Gay 09-17-13

A Vision Inspired By The Heart

A New Day Dawns

For those that know me, that is good,
For those that don't, never understood,
Keep yourself true, Forever and more,
You never know what life has in store.
Go with the flow and do what you know.
Closed within, trying to get out,
One will listen, one will shout,
Emotions of disguises as conflict arises,
In the eyes of the beholder, there is always hope.
No one around, you will learn to cope,
Trials and triumphs will make you stronger.
A true friend will be there and will last longer,
For what lies in your path is what awaits you.
Time will tell for what you go through,
Live with it, deal with it, your time has come,
Make the most of what you can become,
A New Day Dawns, a journey in turn,
For all of this is a lesson to learn…

By: Leanna Gay 09-08-13

A Vision Inspired By The Heart

CHAPTER 8
Inspirations of Art
Art and Photos
By the Author Leanna Gay

Doe and Fawn

Trying to decide

Which way to go.

Picture Taken

By

Leanna Gay

A Vision Inspired By The Heart

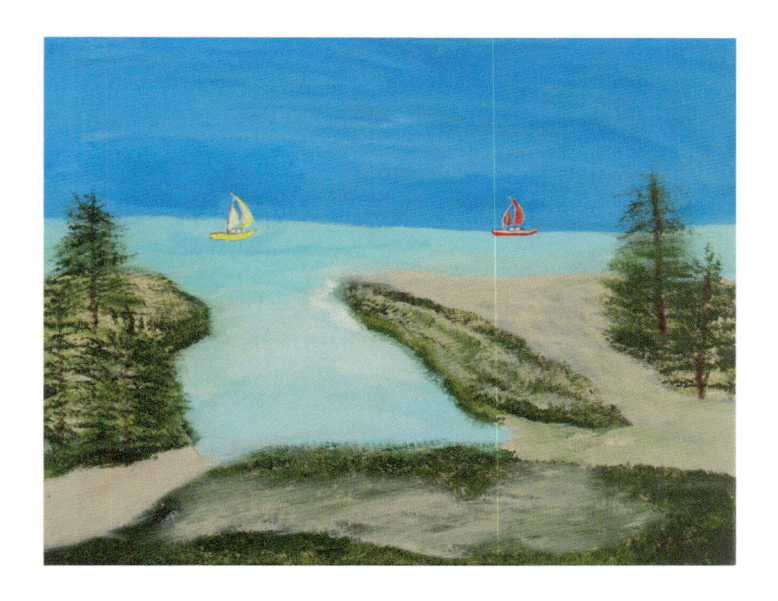

Mystery Bay

Acrylic Painting

By

Leanna Gay

A Vision Inspired By The Heart

TIGER

Strong and Brave.

Acrylic Painting

By

Leanna Gay

A Vision Inspired By The Heart

Mystical Horse

Sunset over looking a mystery lake.

Acrylic Painting

By

Leanna Gay

A Vision Inspired By The Heart

ALBINO LION

Daring to believe.

Strong and Courageous.

Acrylic Painting

By

Leanna Gay

A Vision Inspired By The Heart

Doe and Fawn

Trying to Find Their

Path.

Picture Taken

By

Leanna Gay

A Vision Inspired By The Heart

See & Eye Wolf

Acrylic Painting

By Leanna Gay

Believe in what you see, for what you see

Lies within the eyes of the beholder.

A Vision Of Destiny

ABOUT THE AUTHOR

Leanna Gay started her artistic journey studying ballet and playing the piano since she was 3 years of age. She started writing poetry when she was 9 years of age. After the loss of her mother at age 11, she began to form fictional stories in her mind and by the time she was 13 years of age, she began putting them on paper. She began a new adventure to follow her passion in writing fictional stories. She later found her path and began writing her first series of novels years later. Wife to her best friend of 24 years, Leanna is the mother of 2. She was born and raised in South Georgia, and loves spending her time in the mountains and traveling. Her days are spent writing, exercising, internet marketing and enjoying life with her amazing family.

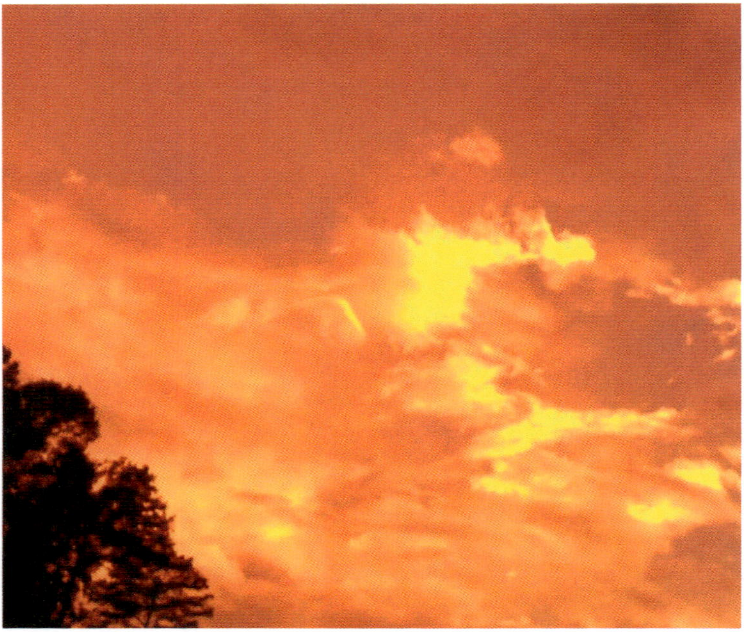

Made in the USA
Charleston, SC
16 February 2014